CRASH COURSE

on the

Old Testament

יקחאתו חתן משה עלה ובחים לאלהים

וכל זקני ישראל לאכל לחם עם חתן

להים : ויהי ממחרת וישב משה

מבר מכס על משה מן הבק

משה את כל אשר

הדבר הזה אשר

משה לבדך וכ

וראם

אלהים

CRASH COURSE

—— on the ——

Old Testament

SIX SESSIONS

CHRISTIANITY TODAY
INTERNATIONAL

BIBLE STUDY

Standard®
PUBLISHING
Bringing The Word to Life
Cincinnati, Ohio

Published by Standard Publishing, Cincinnati, Ohio

www.standardpub.com

Copyright © 2008 by Christianity Today International

Editor: JoHannah Reardon

Creative Development Editors: Kelli B. Trujillo and Roxanne Wieman

Contributing Authors: Bill Barton, Wayne Brouwer, JoHannah Reardon, Marshall Shelley, Kyle White

Cover and interior design: The DesignWorks Group

ISBN 978-0-7847-2246-6

14 13 12 11 10 09 08   9 8 7 6 5 4 3 2 1

CONTENTS

How to Use This Study in Your Group

As Christians, we are a people of the Book. We base most of our knowledge of God and our faith in God on what we read in the Bible. It's critically important that we continually take up our Bibles and pursue a greater understanding of the text and the God who is revealed through it. The goal of the Crash Course Bible Studies series is to help you and your group become more comfortable, knowledgeable, and interested in the Bible—to aid you in that great pursuit of discovering God through his written revelation.

So whether you're a brand-new Christian or a seasoned believer, whether you've read from the Bible every day of your life or are just cracking it open for the first time, you'll find in Crash Course new insights, fresh challenges, and material to facilitate dialogue.

THE OLD TESTAMENT

In this Crash Course Bible study, you'll learn to navigate your way through the Old Testament. We are going to explore what we need to know about this story, and how God wants to use his story to change our lives. The Old Testament is not simply a rule book, a history text, or a collection of spiritual stories with nice morals. It is God's written revelation of himself. We'll approach it as one continuous story, divided into parts to help you understand the order and broad strokes of the story line. The Old Testament is the story of the nation of Israel, told through many individual characters. Understand the personalities and you understand the story. From then on, anything you ever read in the Old Testament can be better understood because you know how the individuals fit into God's continuous plan.

ABOUT THE SESSIONS

Each session in this book is designed for group use—either in a small group setting or adult Sunday school class. The sessions contain enough material to keep your group busy for a full ninety-minute small group time but can also be easily adapted to work in a shorter meeting time—a true crash course. Or if you'd like to spend even more time, feel free to take two weeks for each of the six sessions; that essentially provides a quarter of a year's worth of content for your group.

The readings, activities, and discussion questions will help your group dig deeper into the Bible passages, engage in thought-provoking dialogue, explore ways to personally apply the material . . . and get to know one another better! Every group member should have a copy of *Crash Course on the Old Testament,* both for at-home readings and for use during group time. As you go through the study during your group time, take turns reading aloud the text and questions in the book. That gives everyone a sense of participating in the study together.

Here's how each session breaks down:

Launch

At the beginning of each session, you'll find a great introduction to the topic (be sure to read this aloud at the beginning of your meeting!), a list of Scriptures you'll study during the session, any extra supplies to bring, and notes on anything else to prepare before the session.

There's also a launching activity to start your group time. This activity sets the stage for the week's topic and gets people ready to start talking!

Explore

Next up is the meat of the study—the "Explore" section. This portion includes several teaching points that each focus on a specific aspect of the broader session topic. As you explore each teaching point, you'll study some Scripture passages, interact with one another as you talk through challenging questions, and read commentary on the passages. Also included are excerpts from related Christianity Today International articles (more about that below) that will enrich group discussion. If you are leading the group, be sure to ask God to help you make his Word come alive for your group during this time of exploring his truth (see Hebrews 4:12).

Apply

The Christian life—the abundant life—is about more than just thoughtful study and dialogue. James says, "As the body without the spirit is dead, so faith without deeds is dead" (James 2:26). The "Apply" section of each session will help take your discussion and study to another level; it will help you *live out* the ideas and values from that session. During this time, each participant will choose from three different challenge options (or come up with their own) to do during the coming week. These challenges will help group members make what they've learned a part of their lives in a practical way.

Pray

Before you finish up, be sure to take some time to pray for one another. In the "Pray" section, you'll find an idea you can use for your group's closing prayer.

Before Next Time

Take a look at the "Before Next Time" box for a heads-up on what to read or prepare for your next meeting.

FOR FURTHER RESEARCH

Resource List

Located at the end of session 6 is a list of recommended resources that can help take your study on the topic even further. You'll want to check those out!

Christianity Today International Articles

You'll also find three bonus articles from Christianity Today International publications. These articles are written by men and women well versed in the Old Testament. Each session references one or more of the articles during the course of the study. These articles are meant to help your group dive deeply into the topic and discuss a variety of facts, thoughts, and opinions. Taking the time to read these articles (as well as anything else suggested in the "Before Next Time" box at the end of each session) will greatly enrich your group's discussion and help you engage further with each topic.

It's our prayer that *Crash Course on the Old Testament* will change the lives of your group members as you come to better understand the Old Testament and our God who is revealed there. May the Holy Spirit move in and through your group as you study the Old Testament and seek to live out its timeless messages.

Old Testament Time Line

THE BEGINNING OF TIME

- God creates the world and everything in it, including Adam and Eve. Through Adam and Eve's disobedience, sin enters the world, altering the perfect communion between God and mankind.
- Noah and the flood
- The tower of Babel—God creates distinct languages, causing people to disperse throughout the earth.

2100 BC

- Abraham lives in what is now Iraq. God tells him to move to Canaan, which later became Israel. God promises Abraham great things and numerous descendants. Unlike many people, Abraham believes in the one true God. God rewards Abraham's faith, making him the father of a great nation (Israel).
- Isaac
- Jacob
- Joseph

בריס יי לעם פול הללהים ורבאת ארח

1446 BC

- Moses leads the Hebrew people's exodus to the promised land of Canaan after they have been slaves in Egypt for four hundred years. God gives Moses the law to teach and guide his people.
- The Ten Commandments; golden calf
- Forty years in the desert; the tabernacle
- Joshua and the conquering of the land of Canaan (the promised land)
- The judges Deborah, Gideon, Samson, and others
- Israel's first king, Saul

1010 BC

- David becomes king of Israel and reigns for forty years. David, unlike his predecessor Saul, follows the commands of God. He makes mistakes, but repents of them. He seeks to please God, and God promises David that his heir will sit on a throne forever.
- King Solomon
- The divided kingdom (Israel and Judah)
- The prophets (Isaiah, Jeremiah, Ezekiel, and others)
- God's people sent into captivity (Babylonian and Assyrian Empires)
- God's people return from captivity (Ezra, Nehemiah, Esther)
- Persian supremacy; Alexander the Great
- Four hundred years of silence; Roman occupation of Israel

ויקח יתרו חתן משה עלה ובחים לאלהים

ויבא כל זקני ישראל לאכל לחם עם חתן

האלהים ∴ ויהי ממחרת וישב משה

העם על משה מן הבק

משה את כל אשר

הדבר הוה אשר

לבדך וכל

ויאמ

אליו

The Beginning | 1

Adam and Eve demonstrate the beginning
of God's relationship with mankind.

The story of creation might seem like a small part of the Bible. After all, it's only a handful of chapters. But these chapters are foundational to the whole of the Bible.

The Bible begins with God speaking as "we." God is both I and we, a being in community within himself—a being who is community. God has never been truly alone, even before there was a single entity other than him. The story of the creation of the world starts with a fundamentally, profoundly relational God reaching out into nothing at all to call into being something that will become a reflection of his nature as a being in community.

The world as it was when Adam and Eve first lived in it is not just a prologue or a pipe dream. It is the real world—the original, the true prototype. It's not a fantasy, a fiction, a wish, or a longing.

It is where we came from, a world where everything is harmonious and together—people with themselves, people with the world, people with each other, and people with God. All of existence was one community that was a reflection of the perfect unity and relatedness within the being of God himself. Paradise was a community of complete oneness.

So what happened?

Sin happened—in a way that altered the course of human history for all time.

BIBLE BASIS: *Genesis 1:26-31; 3:1-24*

EXTRA SUPPLIES: *samples of things that are ruined (art or carpentry project, knitting that unraveled, jeans with holes in them, a shredded envelope, a broken vase, etc.)*

BEFOREHAND: *Since this is the first week of your study, the leader should send out an e-mail to everyone in the group. Remind them to purchase their copy of* Crash Course on the Old Testament *if they haven't already. Encourage group members to read the article "The Colorful Creator" by David Shelley on page 71 in preparation for this week's session. And ask everyone to bring in (or think of) a ruined item to share with the group. Be sure to mention where and when you're meeting.*

LAUNCH

Take turns passing around the ruined items and explaining how they got ruined, or tell a story of something you made that was later ruined. Maybe you knitted a magnificent sweater that the dog chewed to pieces, or produced a complex spreadsheet at work that was accidentally deleted. How did you feel when it was ruined? Were you able to fix it? If so, how?

What do you imagine when you think of *paradise*? What images come to mind?

What do you think the original paradise—the Garden of Eden—was like?

Spend a few minutes studying the Old Testament Time Line (p. 10). In looking at the Old Testament as a continuous story, why is the creation story foundational for the rest of the book?

 EXPLORE

Teaching Point One: God established a relationship with mankind at creation.
Read Genesis 1:26-31.

Adam and Eve demonstrate the beginning of God's relationship with mankind. Their story also relates the beginning of sin and the distortion of that perfect community relationship between God and us. But in the beginning God declared it very good. The story of creation implies all sorts of things about the perfect community between God and humans. What are some of the implications about God and mankind that you can glean from this passage?

What are some things that this passage indicates about creation and mankind's perfect relationship to creation?

Describe a time when you really experienced nature. How did you feel? Why do you think nature is able to evoke so many emotions in us?

How does the story of Christianity begin here at creation?

Do you believe that this story of creation is how God really created the earth? Why or why not? Does taking a different position on creation (evolution, the big bang) jeopardize the way we understand God's perfect community? How so? What other positions are there, and what are the implications to the Christian story?

Read the fifth paragraph of the article "The Colorful Creator" (p. 72). What are some ways that creation speaks to you of God's existence?

Teaching Point Two: Humans marred their relationship with God by sinning. Read Genesis 3:1-24.

This heartbreaking account shows the break in the perfect community God had with his people. When was the first time you can remember feeling ashamed for doing something wrong?

What does it mean, they would "be like God, knowing good and evil" (v. 5)?

When God created Adam and Eve, he instilled in them a moral code that came from him. In the snake's deception, Adam and Eve were offered an opportunity to become like God. After they ate the fruit, Adam and Eve knew good and evil. And their moral compasses were no longer rooted in God's character.

Adam and Eve could eat from any tree in the garden except one. God wants us to enjoy and take pleasure in all of his creation. Why is it so hard for humans to enjoy the pleasures God has provided for us and say no to the limitations?

Excuses, excuses! Adam immediately tried to lay the blame for his failure on Eve. Why is taking responsibility for our sins so difficult?

Describe a time when you had trouble owning up to something you'd done. Did you ever admit to it? How did that feel?

In a perfect community, life looked one way; but once sin entered the world, it started to look another way. As a group, use the chart below to describe how aspects of life might have looked in a perfect, godly community compared to how they look now, after the fall.

	Perfect Community	After the Fall
Trust		
Obedience		
Openness		
Ownership		
Blessing		
Fellowship		
Work		
Life		

After sin entered the world, the relationship between God and people *changed,* but it didn't *end.* What does this tell you about God's desire and love for us?

 APPLY

Author Glenn Stanton says, "We serve a God who created our humanity, weeps at the fall of our humanity, became our humanity, and is redeeming our humanity" (www.preachingtoday.com).

If you are following Christ, there may be days that seem to be full of ordinary circumstances. But theologically and truthfully, every day with Christ is an extraordinary day. Right now, you're part of God's redeeming story that is constantly bringing you closer to the perfection you will one day experience with Christ and all other believers. Does this truth shake you? It should.

Choose one of the following application options to do on your own this week. Turn to a partner and share your choice.

CHANGE YOUR ATTITUDE

Tell your partner how you will let this truth (that you're part of God's redeeming story that is constantly bringing you closer to the perfection you will one day experience with Christ and all other believers) change your attitude about your week. Pray aloud with your partner, asking God to use this truth to affect the way you live day-to-day this week. Every night this week, write down one or two ways your day was different as a result of living with the knowledge of this truth. Report back next week about how you did at applying this attitude.

TELL SOMEONE ELSE

Tell your partner the name of one person you know who does not understand that God created him or her for a relationship with him. Make a commitment to tell that person one truth from this study this week. Pray for these people and report back next week about what happened.

CONNECT WITH NATURE

Tell your partner one of your favorite places to go locally to enjoy nature. Make a commitment to go there this week and meditate on the things you have learned in this study. Note the things about nature that are still perfect and good, as well as some things that have been ruined. Report back to your group what you discovered.

PRAY

Wrap up your study by having an expressive reader in your group read Genesis 1 aloud. Imagine it's a soliloquy in a play! After the reading, close in praise to your creator.

BEFORE NEXT TIME: *Finish reading "The Colorful Creator" by David Shelley on page 71 if you have not already done so. For next time, married group members should plan to bring mementos from their weddings, such as the invitation, some photos, or a dried bouquet.*

The Patriarchs | 2

Abraham began a journey of faith
that resulted in the nation of Israel.

*If you've ever had that not-knowing-where-you're-going feeling, then
you can imagine what Abraham felt around three thousand years ago
when he was asked to move to an unknown destination. He left Ur
(Genesis 11:31), which was no Tiny Town. It had walls over sixty feet
thick, perhaps half a million people, indoor bathrooms, fifteen-room
houses . . . even board games. But because Abraham believed God's
word, he was willing to move more than a thousand miles away.*

*According to the Bible, the only way to God is to trust what he
says (John 14:15). In this, Abraham is "the father of all who believe"
(Romans 4:16, NLT). The first use of the word* believe *in the Bible
refers to Abraham (Genesis 15:6).*

In Genesis 12:1-3, the root of the word bless *is used five times. God
blessed Abraham quantitatively, for by 1950, despite the holocaust,*

Abraham had sixteen million descendants. God also blessed Abraham qualitatively. Albert Einstein (scientist), Sandy Koufax (pitcher), and Barbra Streisand (singer) all have something in common. These movers and shakers sprouted from Abraham's family tree.

When God spoke, Abraham responded. He marched forward when God promised him land, and he put up an altar to kill his son at God's command. No wonder that of all the heroes in the Bible's Faith Chapter (Hebrews 11), Abraham gets the most verses for being a faith-full man (vv. 8-19).

(Note: Abraham and Sarah's original names were Abram and Sarai. To keep it simple, we're using the more familiar names in this session.)

BIBLE BASIS: *Genesis 12:1-5; 15:1-6; 22:1-18; Hebrews 11:8-22*

EXTRA SUPPLIES: *wedding mementos, such as invitations, photos, or a dried bouquet*

BEFOREHAND: *The leader should decide when/how to call for the reports on last week's "Apply" options.*

 LAUNCH

Those who brought wedding mementos can share the mementos and tell a little about the hardest part of starting a new life with someone. Or tell of a time you faced a daunting future with little or no guidance. Think about your feelings then and recall the uncertainties that troubled you. Focus particularly on how you prayed during those times. Or if you weren't yet a Christian, where did you turn for direction?

Sometimes we hear the future referred to as "the undiscovered territory." What do you think of that phrase? How have you experienced it in that way?

What road maps have you used to help find a path into this undiscovered territory?

What fears about the future do you have?

 # EXPLORE

Teaching Point One: Abraham acted in faith when God called him to leave his homeland.
Read Genesis 12:1-5 and 15:1-6.

Create a business résumé for Abraham. What were his assets? What were his strengths? What would his personality profile include?

Now imaginatively recreate that first conversation God had with Abraham back in the old country where things were settled and safe (Genesis 12). How might God persuade Abraham to pick up and go? What might Abraham say in response? What were the heated spots in the conversation?

What would Abraham have to know in order to go? What would be the nonnegotiables needed to convince him that this voice in the darkness was more than mere fantasy?

How would Abraham have to talk with Sarah about this? How might other conversations run in the town of Ur? What kind of ridicule might Abraham count on from his family and friends? How might he prepare himself for this?

What rewards do you think pulled Abraham toward the road? What outcomes did he hope for that were larger than the fears and stronger than the uncertainties?

If Abraham were to make a public speech in the marketplace of Ur on the day before he and his troop left, what do you think he would say to seal the deal with those around him? How would he convince them that he was doing the right thing in moving on?

Have you ever given a similar speech, convincing others that God had called you to something, when everyone else just thought you were crazy? What made you do it? How did it turn out?

Teaching Point Two: Abraham acted in faith when God demanded a huge sacrifice.
Read Genesis 22:1-18.

This passage strikes horror in the heart of anyone who is a parent. Why do you think God asked such an outrageous thing of Abraham? And why would Abraham do it?

Read Hebrews 11:19. According to this verse, what was Abraham's faith in God like? How does this kind of faith make trusting God possible in light of such an awful command?

Surely God has never asked such an astounding thing of anyone else throughout history. Why might he have asked this of Abraham at the beginning of establishing his relationship with Israel?

This account creates a picture of what God himself did in giving his Son, Jesus Christ, as a sacrifice for us. What insight does this passage give you into God's love for you?

Teaching Point Three: Abraham's faith story continued through Isaac, Jacob, and Joseph.

Break into three subgroups. Each group should be assigned a different one of the following patriarchs to read about: Isaac (Abraham's son—Genesis 24), Jacob (Abraham's grandson—Genesis 32:22-32), Joseph (Abraham's great-grandson—Genesis 41:15-40). When finished reading, come back together as a larger group and have a spokesperson from each smaller group quickly summarize the passages for the rest of the group.

Read Hebrews 11:8-22.

What were some of the hardships all four generations experienced because of Abraham's obedience to God? What were some of the promises that were fulfilled? According to this passage and the stories you read, how did Abraham, Isaac, Jacob, and Joseph all demonstrate faith?

Trust has its tests. Though God had promised Abraham a giant stretch of land (Genesis 15:18-20), Abraham had to buy a burial plot for Sarah because he didn't own one inch of property (23:16-20). And Joseph ordered that his bones be taken to the promised land when the Israelites left Egypt (although this didn't happen until centuries later; 50:24, 25; Exodus 13:19). As Hebrews 11:13 says, they died without receiving what God had promised.

Read the first paragraph after the heading "Special Revelation: God

Reveals Himself in His Word" in the article "The Colorful Creator" (p. 75). How does the story of the patriarchs demonstrate that "you cannot separate doctrine from story"?

Why do you think faith was such a hallmark of the patriarchs? How did God use their faith to bless generations?

APPLY

The remarkable stories of the patriarchs reveal how important our faith is to God. He wants us to trust him with even the most outrageous things that happen in our lives. He wants us to believe that he loves us, so that we'll keep our faith in him when circumstances collapse around us. Each of us has a unique story to tell about our own faith journeys.

How has your faith been tested? How did you respond to that test? When have you made a "leap of faith" like Abraham's exit from Ur? What happened?

How do you need to trust God right now?

Choose one of the following application options to do on your own this week. Turn to a partner and share your choice.

TRUST GOD WITH YOUR CIRCUMSTANCES

Write down one thing you're having trouble trusting God with. Make a list of ways God has been faithful to you personally in the past, and then take some time to study the Scriptures and find passages that describe God's faithfulness. As you pray this week, meditate on those passages and ask God to remind you of his faithfulness as you take that step of faith and trust God with your issue.

FOLLOW GOD'S CALL

If you know what God is calling you to and need to put feet to it, take some time this week to write about what you need as you travel into "the undiscovered territory." What other people do you want to travel there with, either in direct pilgrimage or moral support? How will you find those people? How will you maintain contact with them? Who will hold you accountable in the journey? How will you know faith from fantasy and trust from stupidity? What resources do you need for the journey? How can our group aid you in finding those resources or being those resources?

 # PRAY

On a scrap of paper, write down one thing in your undiscovered territory (your future) that you're really worried about. Pray silently about what you wrote down. Then as a group, wrap up your prayer by reading Hebrews 11:1 aloud together. Ask God to help each person in the group to have the faith of the ancients—to be sure of what they hope for and certain of what they do not see.

BEFORE NEXT TIME: *Read the Ten Commandments in Exodus 20, and read the article "The Frustration of Doing Good" on page 80. Everyone who has time (and especially the leader) should collect a sample of unusual laws that still exist in U.S. state codes. Find some of these laws by searching "unusual laws" within Web sites like www.helium.com and www.associatedcontent.com. Or do your own general search.*

ויקח יתרו חתן משה עלה ובחים לאלהים

ויבא אהרן וכל זקני ישראל לאבל לחם עם חתן

אלהים : ויהי ממחרת וישב משה

לשפט את העם על משה מן הבקר

משה את כל אשר

הדבר הוה אשר

לבדך וכל

ויאמ

אלהים

The Law | 3

God called Moses to lead his people out of slavery
to the Egyptians and to introduce the law.

*Abraham's great-grandson Joseph rose to a high position in Egypt and
brought his family to live there. However, four hundred years later, the
Israelites had become enslaved to the Egyptians. The Lord used Moses
to help fulfill a long-awaited promise (made to Abraham) to give the
Hebrews a land they could call their own. He also introduced the law to
govern the moral, social, and religious issues of the Hebrew people.*

*By the time Moses showed up on the scene, God seemed to have
been pushed off the face of the earth by everyone, including his own
people. But he still didn't give up on the world. God came to Moses at
the burning bush and called him to continue the movement of people
finding their way back to God. God was being true to his promise
to bring his people into a special place where they could reflect and
represent who God is to the whole world. Moses was a great liberator,*

freeing God's people from slavery. He was also a new kind of leader—one who brought a covenant between God and his people based on law.

Though we are used to thinking of laws as things that restrict and restrain us from doing what we want to do, a loving God gave his people the law as a precious gift, so they could understand the God who had rescued them.

This law is valuable. It guides, heals, protects, and liberates. Many of the laws uphold the preeminence and dignity of God himself. Other laws protect the value and property of people created in God's image. But one thing is certain—this law is a treasure that is meant to direct God's people into living lives that reflect the values of the kingdom of God.

BIBLE BASIS: *Exodus 19:3-8; 20:8; Galatians 3:19-25; 1 Peter 2:9, 10*

EXTRA SUPPLIES: *samples of unusual laws*

 LAUNCH

Take turns reading the unusual laws that were brought in. It seems crazy that these laws still exist in the U.S. state codes, doesn't it? What other seemingly ridiculous laws have you heard of?

Why do we have so many detailed laws at the state and community level?

How do these laws help our society run better? Or do they?

 EXPLORE

Teaching Point One: God is relentless in pursuing a relationship with his people.

When God blessed Abraham, God told him that people who opposed God and wanted to continue in the sinful path that led out of Eden would rise up against God's people. So when Moses led God's people out of slavery homeward to the land promised to Abraham, there was terrific opposition. There was war and battle. There was carnage and slaughter. Much of the time the scenes are hard for us to understand, because the people of God are doing the slaughtering at God's direction. This is no easy thing to grasp, but the trajectory of the story is clear: God is building relationships with those who will come to him through faith. And those who refuse this kind of relationship rise up against God's people.

God's struggle is not just with the people who refuse to recognize him, who reject him. God's own people are stiff-necked and uncooperative. Though God is relentless in his pursuit of a relationship with them, at times it gets ugly. The same God who wiped out his enemies at times strikes out at his own people who oppose him. But the reason is always the same. As hard as God's tough love is to understand, the end is to restore people to a relationship with him as their provider, protector, and leader. God continued to raise up special leaders like Moses to both rescue the people of God and call them to return to him: people like Joshua, Samson, Deborah, and Gideon. The names are different, but the role is the same—to help the people of God find their way back to him. But the people of God continue to resist becoming who God meant them to be.

Read Exodus 19:3-8.

This covenant with Moses and God's people is more conditional than the one God made with Abraham. What was the condition to the promise God gave them in this passage? Why do you think he had this condition?

Absolute promises are dependent upon God's unchanging nature that flows out in love to us, including eternal salvation for those who trust in Christ's redemptive work on the cross. But conditional promises may depend on our behavior. For example, he will carry our burdens *if* we cast them upon him (Matthew 11:28-30), and he will give us his peace that surpasses understanding *if* we trust him (Philippians 4:6, 7).

In Exodus 19:5, 6 God told Moses that Israel would be his "treasured possession," a "kingdom of priests and a holy nation." What do these designations mean?

Peter told his audience the same thing.

Read 1 Peter 2:9, 10.

Sometimes it seems like the easiest way to avoid the dangers of the world is to stay away from them, to retreat. But as Christians we're called to stand out as a light in the darkness—to be in the world but not of it. How have you lived this out in your own life? How have you seen others do this? Give some examples.

Read Exodus 19:8 again.

Bringing people back to God doesn't happen in a vacuum. Together, the entire nation of Israel spoke their response to God. How does it benefit and help unite the community when the entire community sticks to the laws or has the same goal in mind?

What can happen when people in Christian community don't follow the laws of Christ? What are some biblical or personal examples?

Read the first four paragraphs under the heading "Why Did God Give Us the Law?" in the article "The Frustration of Doing Good" (p. 82). What do you think it means that "Indeed I would not have known what sin was except through the law"?

Break into pairs and share two stories: 1) about a time you broke a rule and the consequences of that (even if it was a silly rule), and 2) about a rule you felt was important, so you kept it even under pressure . . . and why. After coming back together, share information (or not) as time allows.

Teaching Point Two: The purpose of the law was to reveal the nature of God and lead us to Christ.

The New Testament expands on the purpose of the Old Testament law given to Moses. When Christ came, he clarified much of the purpose of the law for us. Paul explains it for us in the book of Galatians.

Read Galatians 3:19-25.

According to this passage, what was the purpose of the law? (Note: "Seed" refers to Christ.)

Verse 24 says that the law was put into place so it could "lead us to Christ." When you think of your relationship with Christ, do you think more about rules (laws) or more about grace and faith? Do both faith and rules have their place in the Christian life? Why or why not?

Faith saves, and rules govern our lives. Surprisingly, there are actually more commands in the New Testament than in the Old Testament. Just because we are saved by grace through faith does not mean we can take part in any lifestyle we want. We needed faith to be saved, but God wants us to be made holy by obeying him in response to his love.

There is much freedom in being saved by grace and not by law, but there is also great responsibility to be a positive influence on others. How might a Christian use this freedom for destructive purposes rather than to build up others?

APPLY

The laws of the Old Testament are mostly contained in Exodus (Ten Commandments), Leviticus (sacrificial laws, purity laws), Numbers, and Deuteronomy (laws regarding worship, governing, human relationships). The Old Testament gives more than six hundred commandments that the Israelites were expected to keep. The Old Testament law is still the Word of God for us, even though not all of it is still the command of God to us as it was to ancient Israel. Jesus is the end of the law—he fulfills it. As individuals we need to seek to understand and apply the appropriate commands to our lives today. It's not always cut-and-dried. The same Jesus who apparently overrode the "unclean food" rule in Mark 7:19 and the old priesthood (Hebrews 7–10) also said some serious things about keeping the law (Matthew 5:17-20).

How should Christians today think about and respond to Old Testament laws such as the Ten Commandments (Exodus 20:1-17), dietary and health-related laws (ex: Leviticus 11), and sacrificial laws (ex: Numbers 28, 29)?

The law was given by God to the Israelites as a way to distinguish them as God's chosen people. In the same way, Jesus said that the world will know us as his disciples by our love (John 13:35).

Choose one of the following application options to do on your own this week. Turn to a partner and share your choice.

FULFILL JESUS' COMMAND

Share one strength and one struggle of yours that might communicate to those around you that Jesus Christ lives in you and loves through you. Then commit to at least one idea for demonstrating Christ's love this week (serving in a homeless shelter, visibly showing a more gentle attitude toward a difficult family member, inviting neighbors over for dinner, writing notes of encouragement to coworkers, etc.).

APPLY THE TEN COMMANDMENTS

Read Exodus 20:8 (the fourth of the Ten Commandments). How should that commandment apply to us today? Take some time to write down what God might have intended by giving such a command, and what that might mean to us today. Write down some ways you'd like to commit to keeping the Sabbath holy in your own life.

 PRAY

Skip around in Psalm 119 and see how David felt about God's commands. Pray that God will give you wisdom and insight into what he wants you to obey and learn. Pray also that those in your group will help to represent the love of Jesus Christ to the world around you. Mention some people you would most like to understand the love of Christ.

> BEFORE NEXT TIME: *Read 1 Samuel 16 to prepare for next week's study. The leader should plan to bring two balloons and a pocketknife.*

א ויקח יתרו תהן משה עלה וזבחים לאלהים

אהרן וכל זקני ישראל לאבל לחם עם חתן

אלהים: ויהי ממחרת וישב משה

ויעמד העם על משה מן הבק

משה את כל אשר

הדבר הזה אשר

לבדך וכ

ויאמ

אלהים

The Kings | 4

Saul, David, and Solomon were the
only kings of a unified Israel.

In 1976, presidential campaign spending in the United States for candidates and political parties was $160 million. In 2004, it was $1.2 billion (www.citizen.org). In his song "I Can Explain Everything," producer and songwriter T Bone Burnett questions how anyone can spend so much money every four years for a job that pays considerably less.

We might question some of the actions of modern leaders, but we might also question some of the behavior of the Old Testament kings. Saul, Israel's first king, was a disappointment and met a miserable end. David, the second king, had courageous battles, glorious victories, narrow escapes, unbridled sensuality, flawed humanity, treacherous betrayal, and stunning redemption—all the makings of a summer blockbuster, a story of epic proportion.

There are the stories of defeating Goliath, dozens upon dozens of beautiful psalms, a multitude of victorious battles, mercy shown to treacherous Saul, and the story of fervent worship when David brought the ark of God into Jerusalem. But there are also the stories of David's adultery with Bathsheba, the murder of her husband Uriah, a betraying son, and David's prideful census of his soldiers. He was not a man of perfection, but at the core David had a passionate love for, and reliance upon, God.

When God gave Solomon, David's son and Israel's third king, the opportunity to ask for whatever he wanted, Solomon pleased the Lord by asking for wisdom. God lavished on Solomon "a wise and discerning heart," which surpassed that of anyone who's ever lived (1 Kings 3:12). God also gave him great wealth and honor. Unfortunately, Solomon ultimately misused these great gifts and lost his kingdom as a result.

BIBLE BASIS: *1 Samuel 17; 11:1–12:18; 1 Kings 3, 11; Psalm 51*

EXTRA SUPPLIES: *two uninflated balloons and a pocketknife*

 LAUNCH

The leader should present two uninflated balloons and a pocketknife. Blow into one balloon until it's as full as possible. Tie the balloon. Softly toss the balloon into the air and let it land on the tip of the knife. It will probably pop.

Then inflate the second balloon only about a third to half full and tie it off. Toss it into the air and let it land on the knife. It probably won't pop.

A balloon is more likely to burst when it's fully inflated. How are these two balloons like two people—both of whom may face the same danger, represented by the point of the knife, but one survives unharmed while the other self-destructs?

One of the applications we can take away from this simple object lesson is that we're most at risk when we're most full of ourselves. Read the seventh paragraph under the heading "How Does the Law Cause Our Downfall?" in the article "The Frustration of Doing Good" (p. 84). How does this paragraph reinforce our balloon illustration?

 # EXPLORE

Teaching Point One: David lived before God with passionate trust, even when he failed.

We can tell what we put our trust in, because that's where we have the greatest sense of confidence. How would you complete these sentences: "I feel like I can't be beat when . . ." "I feel best when . . ."

If we derive the most confidence from our position in a company, our bank account, our children's accomplishments, our creative endeavors, our appearance, or our possessions, then our trust is misplaced and on shaky ground. If we can say, as David said, "I come . . . in the name of the LORD" (1 Samuel 17:45), then we have every reason for confidence.

Read 1 Samuel 17.

The story of David and Goliath is usually reserved for the kindergarten Sunday school class. Why? What details surprised you as you read it again?

Where did David place his trust? Discuss all the examples you see. How did that affect his sense of confidence or his attitude? What does this tell you about David and his God? What kind of God uses a boy with a slingshot and no armor to accomplish his purposes?

Read verses 45-48 again. What kind of courage does David's confidence instill in you? When do you need to run "quickly toward the battle line" to meet that which defies God and his people? Is it something in your culture? your community? your home?

Have you ever been surprised to see a child who has just been disciplined turn and jump into his father's or mother's arms and hold on for dear life? Such moments show a contrite and tender heart. They also show a sense of trust, and that the child is more concerned about the relationship than having been caught in a wrong. David's sins are calculated and horrifying, but he runs back to God despite the consequences.

Read 2 Samuel 11:1–12:18.

How does David get from Point A (seeing a woman bathing) to Point B (adultery, deceit, murder, cover-ups, etc.)?

Look how many people were affected by David's lustful action. Besides the toll on David and Bathsheba, there is the blood of Uriah and a number of men in David's army. There is the life of their newborn baby. And David's shameful act causes him to be silent in the face of his sons' acts of rape and murder (2 Samuel 13). There is really no sin that is committed "in secret" (12:12). What does it tell you about God that he would send Nathan to David in this manner?

Read Psalm 51.

Was it arrogant for David to think he could approach God like this after the sin he had committed? How could David pray what he does in verse 4 in light of all the wrecked lives? What does that tell us about all sin?

List all of the requests David made of God in verses 7-12.

What does David say will be the result of his restoration (vv. 13-17)?

In verses 18, 19 why does David bring the whole nation before God?

Teaching Point Two: Solomon started out well but ended disastrously.

When David died, God chose his and Bathsheba's son Solomon to take over. At first, Solomon is humble and somewhat overwhelmed with his responsibilities. In 1 Kings 2, Solomon deals with intrigue, conflict, and conspiracy. He is worried about the security of his scattered and vulnerable nation.

Read 1 Kings 3:1-15.

Most of this passage is a dream sequence. What do you see in these verses that could explain, from a human point of view, why Solomon might have such a dream?

In the dream, God asked Solomon, "What do you want?" Solomon answered by asking for wisdom. God was pleased with Solomon's answer. From your perspective, why was it a good answer? Given his situation, what are some other things he might have been tempted to ask for?

Read 1 Kings 3:16-28.

This is the famous story of Solomon's wisdom being tested. Compare it with other examples in 1 Kings 5:1-7 and 10:1-9. What did Solomon's responses reveal about the kind of wisdom God had given him?

Even as Solomon was starting out very well as a king, do you see any hints of what would eventually lead to his downfall?

Read 1 Kings 11:1-13.

What did Solomon do that caused God to condemn him? How could such a wise man do something like this? How might Solomon have been like the balloon at the beginning of this session? What do you think happened to Solomon's wisdom?

What gifts do you feel God has given you? How have you used those gifts for God's glory (or when will you)? When have you been tempted to use those gifts for your own personal gain against God's wishes?

APPLY

David was "a man after [God's] own heart" (1 Samuel 13:14). It can be a struggle to reconcile this title with the evil David did. But the point of Scripture is not primarily to provide moral role models, but to reveal a sovereign, powerful, satisfying, redemptive, merciful God—a holy God. David's passionate life points us toward a life of trusting, seeking, and worshiping this God. Both Saul and Solomon are a warning to all of us. Starting well doesn't necessarily mean we will finish well. We must diligently guard our spiritual lives.

Choose one of the following application options to do on your own this week. Turn to a partner and share your choice.

EVALUATE YOURSELF

Evaluate your sources of confidence. Have you put your trust in any impostors? If so, what can you do to get back on track?

WRITE A PSALM

Write a psalm to God. Express your passionate heart toward God. Give thanks to him in order to combat discontentment. Not a confident writer? Take one of David's psalms and substitute your own words. If you are musical, put a simple tune to yours or one of David's psalms. Spend some time creatively praising God.

 # PRAY

Silently confess your sins to God and pray for courage to confess to anyone else you have wronged. What sin have you kept secret? Enjoy the restoration you crave from God.

BEFORE NEXT TIME: *If you have a study Bible, read the introductions to the books from Isaiah through Malachi to get an overview of the prophets. Read the article "Preaching the Prophets with Honor" (p. 90).*

... ויק ...והרו תגן משה עלה וזבחם לאלהם

... וכל וקני ישראל לאכל לחם עם חתן

... ולהים: ויהי ממחרת וישב משה

... ויעמד העב על משה מן הבק

... משה את כל אשר

... ודבר הוה איש

... לבק וי

... ויאמ

... אלהים

...

...

The Prophets | 5

Proclaimers of hope or predictors of doom?

After Solomon's death the nation of Israel divided into the northern and southern kingdoms. The people, in general, continued to flirt with and even adopt the false religions of those around them. The prophets were given the task of warning citizens of both kingdoms of their impending doom if they did not repent. Unfortunately, the people didn't listen, and they suffered the consequences. The northern kingdom (Israel) was conquered first by Assyria in 722 BC. The southern kingdom (Judah) fell to Babylon in 586 BC.

The prophets were holy men moved by the Holy Spirit to foretell things that would come to pass—things that humans could not figure out on their own. The purpose of their prophecies was always to reveal God's character and his relationship to his lost people. So although they preached doom, they also preached reconciliation and restoration.

LAUNCH

One volunteer will role-play being a "prophet" to the rest of the group. The prophet will imagine that he or she has a message from God. The message can be whatever the actor chooses. Perhaps this imaginary word from God would include the group's taking a trip to Haiti and doing street evangelism to people there. Or make it silly—maybe it would be that everyone has to quit eating chocolate. Use your imagination and do your best to persuade the group they need to do this. Be passionate and determined. The group can respond in any way this message makes them feel.

How did you feel when the prophet was telling you what to do? Did it make you mad? Did it make you laugh? Were you tempted to take your prophet seriously?

How might this be similar to how the Israelites felt when the prophets were telling them what to do? How might it be different?

Read "The Prophet Calls for Communion with God" in the article "Preaching the Prophets with Honor" (p. 93). Do you think there are any modern-day prophets? If so, who might they be? What is their message? Consider also the other tasks the Old Testament prophets had—reproving and admonishing the wicked, and comforting and consoling the righteous, for example. What are today's prophets doing? How might we benefit from their message?

 EXPLORE

Teaching Point One: The prophets were reviled while they lived.

The prophets had the difficult task of telling their people a message they didn't want to hear—that God was going to judge the nation for their sin, which would result in exile and captivity.

Read Isaiah 57:15-21.

Why must God punish sin? How does he feel about punishment? Why did he give Israel a second chance (and a third and a fourth . . .)?

Read Jeremiah 2:26-30; 5:3-5 and Luke 4:24-27.

Why do people tend to ignore or disbelieve prophets? What are the consequences of that?

Read Jeremiah 20:7-18; Ezekiel 2:3-6; 3:1-9; Amos 7:14, 15 and Habakkuk 2:6-11.

How did the prophets feel about their callings?

What hazards of the prophet's life did God warn Ezekiel about?

What were Amos's roots, and how may that have influenced his words to Israel?

What sins was Habakkuk concerned about? What was his style of delivery?

Teaching Point Two: God convicted and condemned his people through the prophets' words.

Although many of God's words through the prophets sounded harsh, God used the prophets to proclaim how far Israel had fallen from God's perfect plan for them. God wanted his people to remember him, to stop trying to replace him with idols, and to understand the consequences of turning away from him.

Read Amos 8.

To whom does Amos direct his prophecies? For what time periods do they seem to be given?

What "day" is Amos talking about? When have God's people experienced a famine of "hearing the words of the LORD"? (v. 11). How does the meaning of the passage change when we read it as though it were directed toward us today?

What moral perspective on man's deeds did Amos give?

How did God and the Israelites differ on what was right and wrong and the seriousness of their actions?

What cosmic view of history do we find in this passage?

What do we learn about God from Amos's words? It is difficult to know what period(s) of time Amos is addressing. Which truths in the passage are timeless?

Teaching Point Three: God offered hope and redemption through the prophets' words.

God did not use the prophets to preach only doom and gloom for his people. God also spoke through the prophets of his redemptive plan, hope, and ultimate delivery. God often used the prophets to remind the Israelites that he was with them and for them.

Read the section "The Prophet Points Out God at Work" of the article "Preaching the Prophets with Honor" (p. 92).

Read Isaiah 42:8; Jeremiah 17:10; Lamentations 3:31-33 and Nahum 1:2, 3.

What does God want us to know about himself?

What does he want from us? What makes him angry and what delights him?

How do you balance God's words in these passages with the harshness of his words in previous passages?

How do these verses show God's love for us?

 APPLY

Choose one of the following application options to do on your own this week. Turn to a partner and share your choice.

LEARN FROM THE PROPHETS

Journal your thoughts on the following: What have you learned about God as you read verses from the prophets? What have you learned about yourself? In what ways might studying the books of the prophets enhance your spiritual growth?

BECOME A PROPHETIC GROUP

Get together with several people from your group or church to discuss some practical ways you can have a prophetic ministry to the world. Review your notes and list some of the ways the prophets were used by God. What can your group or church do to encourage Christians to develop a mind-set that understands the importance of staying true to God?

PRAY

Dim the lights in the room. One of the most important tasks some of the prophets had was to bring the news of the coming Messiah. Have a volunteer read aloud Isaiah 9:6, 7 and 11:1-5. Spend a few moments in silent prayer, honoring God for his greatest of all gifts.

BEFORE NEXT TIME: *Read Daniel 1 and Nehemiah 1 to prepare for next week's session. The leader should plan to bring a stack of newspapers and news magazines (for information on disasters and injustice).*

ויקח יתרו חתן משה עלה וזבחים לאלהים

כל זקני ישראל לאכל לחם עם חתן

להים ׃ ויהי ממחרת וישב משה

על משה מן הבק

משה את כל אשר

הדבר הוה אשר

משה לבדך וכ

ויא

The Exile and Return | 6

Daniel, Ezra, and Nehemiah remained
faithful to God and his Word.

After the southern kingdom fell, its citizens were taken into captivity. By looking at the book of Daniel, we gain insight into what this was like. This book carries a big megaphone. The message God has for us? "You are not in control! I am the sovereign Lord." God highlights this announcement with powerful dreams, dramatic rescues, stunning retributions, and mysterious prophecies. In the center of this is Daniel, an out-of-town slave boy turned right-hand man to the king of Babylon. And why not? The story is covered in the unmistakable fingerprints of God. So much so that even a self-worshiping king is moved to declare reverence for God: "He is the living God and he endures forever; his kingdom will not be destroyed, his dominion will never end" (6:26).

The story of Daniel continues to move us to worship the everlasting, sovereign God and allows us to be his uncompromising, bold, and devoted servants in the face of a corrupt culture.

Ezra and Nehemiah, who lived later than Daniel, were part of the joyous return to Jerusalem after years of captivity. Ezra supervised the rebuilding of the temple, and Nehemiah the rebuilding of the city walls. Together they represent a new beginning.

BIBLE BASIS: *Daniel 5; Nehemiah 1:1-11; 8:1-12*

EXTRA SUPPLIES: *newspapers and news magazines*

 # LAUNCH

Break into groups of three or four. Each group should look through a newspaper or news magazine to find an article that represents a disaster or injustice. Then discuss together the negative emotions you would feel if you were living through that catastrophe.

Which of the following best describes your reaction in the midst of hardship?

- ❏ I thank God in the middle of the difficulty.
- ❏ I rail at God because he seems unfair.
- ❏ I thank God after the crisis is over.
- ❏ I despair because I lose hope.
- ❏ Other: _____

Why do you think you react this way?

בָּרֲכוּ יָם כִּי לְעוֹלָם חַסְדּוֹ הַלְלוּ אֶת

How can you learn to thank God in the middle of difficulty, knowing he is wise and loves you? How would you find hope in the middle of such an ordeal? What would keep you from despair?

 EXPLORE

Teaching Point One: God gave Daniel confidence, even though he lived in exile under unreasonable kings.

Have you ever noticed how readily people offer their opinions and criticisms in private, but when it comes time to voice those concerns to those who need to hear them, those same closet critics take a vow of silence? The storyteller Aesop wisely observed, "It is easy to be brave from a distance" (www.wiseoldsayings.com). Sadly, fear often prevents us from speaking up when it would make a world of difference. Daniel modeled a boldness that could be traced directly to confidence in God's sovereignty. In fact, he was able to tell a king to his face: "The Most High God is sovereign over the kingdoms of men. . . . But you . . . have not humbled yourself, though you knew all this. Instead, you have set yourself up against the Lord of heaven" (Daniel 5:21-23).

Read Daniel 5.

What does verse 17 tell you about our man Daniel? What does it tell you about his faith and his God?

What kinds of risks did Daniel take by speaking so boldly?

In what ways do you see God's sovereignty in this chapter?

Daniel showed that he believed devotion to God was more valuable than life itself. How does that belief surface in your life?

Teaching Point Two: God gave Ezra and Nehemiah courage to begin again.

Nehemiah lived in exile because his homeland was conquered by the Babylonians, who were then conquered by the Persians. Fortunately, the Persians later allowed many of the Jews to return to Jerusalem. At this point the temple had been rebuilt under Ezra's leadership, but the city walls were still in ruins. Nehemiah wanted to rebuild the walls, so his first actions were to fast and pray. And what a prayer! He knew who he was putting his confidence in as he spent time praising God for being great and awesome. He also knew that Jerusalem was in disrepair because of the nation's disobedience, so he confessed that shortcoming.

Read Nehemiah 1:1-4.

In the time period during which Nehemiah lived, a city needed walls to survive raids from neighboring kingdoms. Without walls, it was helpless. It would be similar to living in a house you couldn't lock today. Why do you think hearing that the walls were in disrepair was so devastating to Nehemiah?

Why would Nehemiah care about Jerusalem even though he'd never been there?

בָּרָא מִן לְעַם סֹֹּ אֱלֹהִים הַשָּׁלוֹם וְהָאָרֶץ אֶת

Read Nehemiah 1:5-11.

Nehemiah delighted in who God is and felt remorse about his own sin. Why would it have helped Nehemiah's faith to recount to God what he knew about him (v. 5)? How could this practice help you?

What might Nehemiah's prayer tell us about the importance of taking responsibility for the sin of the society or group we are a part of, even if we have not personally committed the sin (v. 6)? What are some sins we should confess for our church, race, community, or country?

Teaching Point Three: God wanted Israel's worship and fellowship, just as from the beginning.

Read Nehemiah 8:1-12.

All of life is worship. When Ezra read and explained God's law to the people, they caught this vision. They listened to God's Word (8:3) and then responded with their bodies (8:5, 6), their voices (8:6), and their tears (8:9). Their worship included confession (9:3), prayer (9:4), and praise (9:5). Old Testament rituals involved entire families in order to instruct children in the story of God's great salvation. In the same way, their worship extended into the neighborhoods as they "went away to eat and drink, to send portions of food and to celebrate with great joy, because they now understood" (8:12).

What a great day in Israel's history! The nation valued the Word of God so much that they assembled their families to hear it read. And when they realized all the ways they had sinned against a holy God, they repented and then rejoiced that they finally understood what was expected of them.

The shape of worship today will differ from that of Ezra's day. While you may not throw dirt on your head to show sorrow for your sins or build a shelter out of branches on your roof, you still must allow God's Word to capture all your being and permeate all your living—because God is greater than mere words can express!

How long did this public reading last (v. 3)? Why would they be willing to listen for so long? What does that tell us about their respect for God's Word?

What was the significance of the people of Israel standing when Ezra began to read the Word of God (v. 5)? What was the significance of lifting their hands and finally bowing down in worship (v. 6)? What difference does our posture make in our attitude? What does that mean for us today?

How do you usually respond to a clear command from Scripture?

❑ I ignore it.
❑ I fight God on it, then eventually give in.
❑ I try to obey it by God's power.
❑ I rationalize it.
❑ Other: _____

Why do you think you react this way?

Read the third paragraph under the heading "Special Revelation: God Reveals Himself in His Word" in the article "The Colorful Creator" (p. 76). What reason is suggested in this paragraph for why we ignore God's Word?

APPLY

Daniel, Ezra, and Nehemiah all trusted God in the middle of difficult circumstances. They believed his promises and clung to them, even when their situations seemed impossible. We too can respond with such faith to God in our circumstances.

Choose one of the following application options to do on your own this week. Turn to a partner and share your choice.

EXAMINE YOUR DEVOTIONAL LIFE

Perhaps you need to break up some dry ground regarding your Bible reading and prayer times. Some books that might be helpful are the classic writings of C. S. Lewis, Oswald Chambers, and A. W. Tozer. Perhaps you could pray or read your Bible in a new location. Stand before God while reading his Word. Read a short passage of Scripture in three different versions. Take a prayer walk around your neighborhood or the mall, silently praying for anyone you meet. Also ask around your church or small group for others' devotional ideas.

ACT BOLDLY

What situations require your boldness right now? What risks are involved? What would it look like for you to acknowledge God's sovereignty in those situations? Tell your group what you need to move ahead on and ask for their prayers and encouragement. Take some time this week to pray more about this and write down steps you can take to make progress. For bold and serious prayer, prostrate yourself on the floor.

PLAN A NIGHT TO CELEBRATE GOD'S SOVEREIGNTY

Get together with a group of friends, brew some coffee, and have a time of testimony. Recount how God was at work even before you knew him, and how he has been moving since the time you decided to follow him. Let everyone share. You might be surprised at how often we don't know each other's faith histories and how powerful these testimonies are. Then have a time of repentance for the ways pride and fear have crept into your lives. Invite the group to be on its knees—a good posture in light of God's sovereignty. End with a time of worshiping the sovereign, good God together.

 # PRAY

Practice some of the methods the Israelites used in the passage we read in Nehemiah. Ask the group to stand while someone reads Psalm 101. When that person is finished, instruct the group to raise their hands and call out "amen," which means "so be it." Spend some time in either public or private confession.

FOR FURTHER RESEARCH

Note: The Crash Course series is designed to help you study important topics easily. The following books and magazine articles present additional valuable research. Items in the resource list are provided as a starting point for digging even deeper. Not everything in "For Further Research" is necessarily written from a conservative evangelical viewpoint. Great discussion and real learning happen when a variety of perspectives are examined in light of Scripture. We recommend that you keep a concordance and Bible dictionary nearby to enable you to quickly find Bible answers to any questions.

RESOURCE LIST

Survey of the Old Testament, Gleason Archer (Moody Publishers, 2007). Thoroughly covers such issues as creation, the flood, authorship, and chronology.

A Popular Survey of the Old Testament, Norman L. Geisler (Baker Academic, 2007). Illustrated survey with color photos, charts, and maps. Written in an easy, informal style.

God of New Beginnings: Brief Insights from Genesis & Exodus, W. E. McCumber (Beacon Hill Press, 1991). A devotional look at great persons and events from the first two books of the Bible.

The Magnificent Obsession: Knowing God As Abraham Did, Anne Graham Lotz (Zondervan, 2008). Personal anecdotes, unforgettable stories, and inspirational insights help you relate to God as Abraham did—as a close friend.

The Pentateuch (Old Testament, Volume Three in the Standard Reference Library, Standard Publishing, 2008). Takes the reader from Eden to Canaan, from the creation of the universe to the creation of a nation.

Free to Love: Looking at the Law Through Jesus' Eyes, Timothy E. White (Tate Publishing, 2008). Christianity exists in two very distinct camps—one emphasizes the devastating effects of sin, while the other emphasizes the deliverance of the Savior, thereby canceling the power of the other.

The Prayers of David: Becoming a Person After God's Own Heart, Baker Publishing Group (Bethany House, 2007). Powerful, life-changing secrets from David's life and journey with God help readers in their own journeys.

Poetry and Prophecy (Old Testament, Volume Five in the Standard Reference Library, Standard Publishing, 2008). Examines some of the favorite passages in the Old Testament.

Introduction to Old Testament Prophetic Books, C. Hassell Bullock (Moody Publishers, 1986). Get a clear picture of Israel's history, as well as sharper understanding of Old Testament prophets and prophetic literature.

The History of Israel (Old Testament, Volume Four in the Standard Reference Library, Standard Publishing, 2008). Surveys the events of Israel's history from the crossing of the Jordan to the exile beyond the Euphrates.

Return from Exile: The Smart Guide to the Bible Series, Daymond R. Duck; Larry Richards PhD, editor (Thomas Nelson, 2008). Ezra, Nehemiah, Haggai, and Zechariah can speak volumes to the current situation of the church and the future that is ahead in the return of Christ.

The Colorful Creator

Don't miss the creative wonder of the Artist's masterwork.

by David Shelley

I grew up in a family that never had a color television set. All the ballgames and TV shows—including the "Wonderful World of Disney"—were in shades of black and white. As a Christmas gift a few years ago, my kids gave me a set of videos about professional football in the 1960s—the era I grew up in. After I watched one of them, the whole family laughed at my naiveté when I said, "I had no idea football uniforms were so colorful back then. My memories of them are in black and white."

Do you live in color? Or is your existence—especially your spiritual life—a mean and uninteresting acknowledgment of a bad news, black-and-white God? Our concept of the Lord, our salvation, and the message of the gospel may be as dull and unattractive as my memories of football in the '60s. We need to awaken to the colorful reality of our multi-dimensional, breathtaking, unpredictable Creator, who is not vague, but specific, not demeaning, but expansive. This is truly Good News that changes everything.

One problem common to Christians is the tendency to make the gospel sound decidedly grim, hopeless, and unappealing. This has happened throughout the 2,000-year history of the church. This happens in a lot of well-intentioned sermons that make it sound as if the burden is entirely on your shoulders, and if you'd just straighten up and do a few impossible things, then God would call you his own.

Fortunately, the Lord in whom we live and move and have our being, who created us and continually sustains us, has revealed himself to us as the beautiful, creative, soul-enriching, transcendent, breathtaking God he really is. In other words, God, the Sovereign Creator, is the colorful Reality in which we receive and live out the gospel. Without trusting the Sovereign Lord and enjoying the Creative Lord, we can neither fully experience nor fully communicate his gospel. Because God has revealed himself to everyone through creation (general revelation) and to his people through his Word (special revelation).

GOD REVEALS HIMSELF IN CREATION

Before God ever made known the specifics of his character and his purposes, he revealed himself through his creation. We do not begin existence as abstract truths comprehended by disembodied minds. We grow in awareness through physically experiencing the wonders of creation—sound, light, shape, color, motion, smell, and taste. The more we learn about our world, the more wondrous it seems that the planet should sustain life at all. It requires the perfect properties of water and atmosphere in the essential proportions, the exact gravitational pull, the precise speed of the planet's rotation, the ideal distance from the sun, and a host of other necessities for physical life to exist. Change any of these factors and we all die. "The heavens declare the glory of God," the psalmist says in Psalm 19:1-3. "The skies proclaim the work of his hands. Day after day they pour forth speech; night after night they display knowledge. There is no speech or language where their voice is not heard."

The stars have always mystified us, and the more we know about them, the more expansive is our wonder at their Creator. With all our knowledge of cellular biology, subatomic physics, and the nature of light itself, we are increasingly impressed by the masterful complexity pointing to a super-intelligent Designer. In a culture that has made every effort to reduce the wonders of nature to scientific data, why is it that the unexplainable beauty of a flower, a sunset, or a storm can still take our breath away?

Two things should be obvious in light of all the artistry around us. First, there is a higher knowledge—a superior reality behind it all. Second, his power is beyond limit.

When Job demanded an explanation from God for what he had suffered, how did the Lord answer? He spread before him the wonders of creation: "Where were you when I laid the earth's foundation? . . . Have you journeyed to the springs of the sea or walked in the recesses of the deep? . . . Have you seen the gates of the shadow of death?" (Job 38:4, 16, 17). He goes on in magnificent poetry, flashing images of light, snow, hail, lightning, desert, frost, constellations, wild beasts, and even the birthing process. This overwhelming display of the wonders of creation causes Job to reply, "I didn't know what I was talking about; I'll shut up and listen" (Job 40:4, 5, paraphrase). Later Job acknowledges, "I know that you can do all things; no plan of yours can be thwarted. . . . Surely I spoke of things I did not understand, things too wonderful for me to know" (42:2, 3).

Like Job, the psalmists, the Prophets, and even Jesus call forth praise for the wonders of creation. It is abundantly evident that such a Creator is in no way my inferior, nor could I reasonably conclude that he is small-minded, petty, or a killjoy.

One summer, my dad, brother, and I took a family history exploration through the American southeast. We had seen Jamestown, where John Shelley arrived in 1622, and we were heading south into North Carolina, where the Shelleys farmed in the 1700s. Dad wanted to head straight for Edenton along the wilderness path that our forefathers would have traveled. But my brother, Marshall, and I wanted to see the barrier islands of near-tropical dunes between the Atlantic Ocean and Albemarle Sound—where the English first attempted to establish American colonies. Marshall and I prevailed, because Marshall was driving and we outnumbered Dad.

When we climbed out of our air-conditioned rental car at a public parking lot in Kitty Hawk, we noticed that every home on the island was built from the second story up. What we would call the first story was a series of 8x8 stilts, constructed as attempts to minimize the damage from storm surges caused by the hurricanes that frequent those islands. So before we ever saw the waves, we saw evidence of the awesome power of nature and of human attempts to deal with that power as a fact of life.

In the 100-degree heat, under an oppressive afternoon sun, we climbed a boardwalk over the 12-foot dunes, between sea grasses and wind-blown palm trees, and came in sight of that vast horizon of rolling waters we call the Atlantic Ocean. Few sights in life can compare to the humbling effect of gazing across the unknown depths and distances of the ocean. As Dad snapped photos and Marshall and I kicked off our shoes and waded in the first few inches of those awesome, green depths, the salt wind whipped our faces, the sand gave way under our cooling feet, and I thought of the exotic places this ocean could take me. I thought of the multi-shaped masterpieces that swim in its dark world below the surface and the people who walked these shores centuries ago. I thought of the Creator who conceived it all, sustains it all, and still cares specifically about me, a speck on a speck of his universe.

I prayed, "Lord, You grant blessings like this to take my breath away; free me from my chronic proneness to be nearsighted and petty—to treat insignificant things as though they were big and great things as though they were small." Creation overwhelmed me with the awareness of a Master Artist who made all this in awe-inspiring detail—someone so great and powerful that he could sustain every molecule; someone so intimate that he knows me inside and out; someone so unlimited that he cares about a nobody like me, along with every other nobody in his marvelous creation.

Where did I get the imagination to see these invisible realities? I've been to aquariums in Chicago and Monterey and San Diego, so I've seen colorful wonders that inhabit the unseen deep. I've seen the glimpses of Earth brought to us by the Hubble telescope, so I have an inkling of the colors of the cosmos. I've read captivating stories of people over the millennia, and I've traveled to many of the places where they lived, so I have a connection that transcends time. But I could make these vivid connections with unseen things as I stood on the Outer Banks for two reasons: a wonderful imagination I inherit as a man made in the image of a Creator, and his special revelation. Paul explained it this way in Acts 17:24-28: "The God who made the world and everything in it is the Lord of heaven and earth and does not live in temples built by hands. . . . From one man he made every nation of men, that they should inhabit the whole earth; and he determined the times set for them and the exact places where they should live. God did this so that men would seek him and perhaps reach out for him and find him, though he is not far from each one of us. 'For in him we live and move and have our being.'"

Our God is the God of wonders. Don't turn his amazing story into a mere math problem. Don't present the gospel as though God were petty. Instead, proclaim his glory. The Lord whose gospel we proclaim is the source of the beauty and wonder that inspire us. Don't miss the creative wonder of the Artist's masterwork.

SPECIAL REVELATION: GOD REVEALS HIMSELF IN HIS WORD

It is no minor thing that God has spoken to us in words. The ancients believed that language, both the spoken and written word, was our direct link to the divine element that gives meaning to all of life. The Bible comes from the same perspective. According to John 1:1-3, God made himself known to us by means of his *logos*, his Word. By his Word God created all things.

Not only are we dependent upon God's Word for existence; we are further dependent upon God's Word for the meaning and purpose in our existence. When we ignore the Word of the Creator, we shut ourselves off from our source and, therefore, from our very purpose in being.

Before I explain what God's Word is, I need to point out what it is not. First, it is not dry, abstract doctrine, disconnected from real life. Every part of Scripture is inseparably rooted in time-and-place situations of actual people. God did not choose to make himself known as a formula conceivable only in abstraction. He's a personal being who calls other personal beings so that they might know him. In other words, you cannot separate doctrine from story. The minute we take the living, active Word of God and filter it through an abstract principle, we risk filtering out the very life the Word brings.

If God's Word is not abstract doctrine disconnected from real life, what is it? God's Word is story. It is the record of the actions of God in direct relation to his people. It is the workings of God in the material world, in human history—in meaningful interaction with his creation. That is, God has made himself known to us not only through his material creation (general revelation), but also more specifically through his direct, personal, and verbal communication (special revelation).

Nevertheless, we tend to drift away from reading the Bible as he has given it to us and begin to read it as a reference tool—like a dictionary or a phone book. When you treat God's Word that way, you dissect it and end up taking what you want and ignoring the rest. Perhaps worse, you think of the whole as nothing more than a list of facts or regulations, and you become blind to the overarching work of God through the history of his interaction with his people. That is to say, the form in which God gave us his Word is not accidental. He could have written it more like the DMV handbook, and right and wrong would have seemed easier for us to understand. But then we wouldn't really know what God is like; we would have clear rules, but not a vital relationship. God in his wisdom determined that the whole story was necessary in order for us to know and follow him.

The Bible opens in Genesis with poetry. Every stanza begins, "And God said." Each stanza ends, "And there was evening, and there was morning—the first day" (second day, third day, etc). It has rhythm, form, and flow. The content is a tidy summary of the wonders of all creation. The Lord summarizes creation, but he does not trivialize it. On the contrary, we're the ones who tend to take the wonder out of the text by turning it into an argument instead of enjoying the awesome wonder of all that God has made.

The Bible ends with Revelation 21 and 22, passages full of light and color, sound and action, and beauty beyond description. The Revelation is written in the most intricate of poetic literature to vividly contrast the horrors of our fallen world with the glories of Christ's reign. The opening and closing passages of the Bible emphasize the unending, extravagant wonders of our Creator—whom we risk portraying as a grumpy old man, griping about the irresponsibility of kids these days and threatening to sell the lot of us for dog food if we don't start pulling our weight.

Between Genesis and Revelation, the Lord unfolds a story of real people in real places who learn to deal with real struggles in their relationship with God in a fallen and broken world. In the process, the Lord calls a man named Abraham and establishes a covenant relationship with him. Theirs is not an impersonal, take-it-or-leave-it contract, but a through-thick-and-thin kind of relationship. The thin times show up in vivid drama: Abraham leaves the greatest civilization on the planet to wander in the wilderness; Jacob runs for his life; Joseph is falsely accused and thrown into an Egyptian prison; salvation is displayed to an enslaved people, who, once led into freedom, gripe and demand to return to slavery.

There are also five books of pure poetry that grapple with the mysteries of suffering, human passion, and practical living. This poetry gives us a language for talking with God. He uses the most artistic of human language to express the deepest of our relational dynamics.

The Psalms call us 36 times to sing. A third of those songs are psalms of complaint dealing with grief, suffering, and the human struggle to understand. The Prophets turn the conversation around. Using the most powerful and colorful poetry, God now pours out his heart to stubborn, self-destructive people. He uses graphic images—a man beaten beyond recognition; a heart of flesh replacing a heart of stone; dry bones brought to life; a faithless harlot brought home as wife again; a refiner's fire—all express with literary passion God's relentless heart for his beloved people.

The gospel is there, over and over again, but it is not delivered like a systematic theology text. It's there in poetic language, beautiful language, heart wrenching, and graphic language. God does not deliver his Word like some secret *Da Vinci Code* for later generations to decipher; he delivers it in language that cannot be ignored by real people in real and perilous circumstances, facing apathy, idolatry, oppression, and destruction.

Ultimately God spoke his Word not only through human literature, but in human flesh. As John 1:14 explains, "The Word became flesh and made his dwelling among us. We have seen his glory, the glory of the One and Only, who came from the Father, full of grace and truth."

The four Gospels are called "Gospels" because they record the event of God's entrance onto the human stage. The gospel is not a fantasy with make-believe names and places; nor an allegory of a symbolic messiah figure. Rather, the four Gospel writers went to great pains to demonstrate that the baby Jesus was born in Bethlehem, Judea, during the reign of Caesar Augustus, while Quirinius was governor of Syria. By adulthood he was known as "the carpenter's son" (Matthew 13:55) in Nazareth, Galilee. He lived with, taught, and carried out his actions in relationship with Matthew, Peter, John, and James—people who were still testifying as first-hand witnesses when the Gospels were written.

We dare not lose sight of the fact that God has revealed himself to us in a wonderful story in which he is the main character. Now that character has a face, hands and feet and scars, and a name to be proclaimed again and again. Don't turn this amazing story into a mere formula. Don't present the gospel as if it were unrelated to real life. The Lord, whose gospel we proclaim, captivates and defines us. Don't miss the creative wonder of the Artist's masterwork.

CONVERSION AND INDWELLING: GOD REVEALS HIMSELF IN RELATIONSHIP

Robert Culver gives this account in *The Living* God: "A woman in a tribe that had never heard the gospel listened as a missionary told the wonderful story to her for the first time. She looked at the missionary and said, 'I always thought there ought to be a God like that.'"

The Good News is there *is* a God like that. He's the source of every beauty and pleasure you've ever dreamed of. He's the main character in whose story your story can find its ultimate meaning. That's why you need to hear the story and live the story for yourself. It's at this point that everyone runs into a wall: You can't know and live the story alone. By yourself you won't get it—you won't know him until he makes himself known personally in you. Without a personal relationship with the source, you can only believe an abstraction. Abstraction is not the same thing as knowing him personally.

Through the special revelation of God's written Word, God effectually calls us into his life. Remarkably, he calls us to call on him. If you respond to his Word by calling on him as your Savior and Lord, you will be saved. But don't imagine the life of faith to be a mere concept or religion. The Lord—whose gospel we proclaim in the Savior—indwells and transforms his people. Don't miss the creative wonder of the Artist's masterwork.

The Frustration of Doing Good

*The apostle Paul eloquently explains how the law
causes us to do the very things we don't want to do—
clearly accentuating our need for grace.*

by Paul Borden

Most Americans see themselves as flexible, innovative, and open to change. Contrary to the people who live in the Old World, we see ourselves as having a pioneering spirit. If there's a job out there that needs to be done, if there are changes that need to be made, we perceive ourselves as the kind of people who will do that.

Yet even though we see ourselves as people of change, we often resist change that is imposed upon us. If we are initiating it, if we are creating it, then we are for change. But when someone else is imposing it, we tend to be more rigid.

Perhaps it's because we see change that is imposed as being inefficient or inconvenient. Recently my wife had some cabinets moved in the kitchen. Aesthetically it makes the kitchen look a lot better. But I must now walk four extra steps to get that bowl for my ice cream. I'm not sure I like that kind of change.

When it comes to the church, we are no different. We have the idea that if God and his Word are eternal, then that which we have done in the past should continue on for eternity. But perhaps the biggest reason we resist change is that we see change as a commentary on the past. If we are making a change in what we do, we often assume that implies what we have done in the past is somehow inferior, inadequate, perhaps even wrong. And we have committed our lives and our service to Jesus Christ by doing whatever for the last five or ten or fifteen years, something someone has now said is inferior.

Sometimes that is true, but often it isn't. Many times changes come because the original idea, the original method, has met its purpose. New purposes have arisen, new goals have come, and therefore changes must be made. Change is not so much a commentary on the inferiority of the past; it's just a matter of a different purpose.

THE APOSTLE PAUL IMPOSED A MAJOR CHANGE: LIVE BY GRACE, NOT BY THE LAW.

In the Book of Romans, Paul introduced a major change. He told them to live by grace, not by the law.

For 1,500 years, from the time God had given the law to his nation, men and women of God assumed the way to live, the way to be a nation, the way to be holy, the way to serve God, was to keep the law. Paul came along and said, "Live by grace." That's a major change.

Now what Paul said is crucial for you and me. For 2,000 years the church has struggled with the change Paul suggested. We look at the Ten Commandments, we look at the law of God, and somehow we have the idea that law is still good. It's still from God. It should have a relationship to us today if we are serving the same God, who is eternal. Therefore, we often misunderstand the purpose for law, and wonder why Paul says in Romans to make a change, live by grace.

WHY DID GOD GIVE US THE LAW?

It's imperative that we understand why God gave the law. Paul wants to tell us that purpose, and then by way of illustration, point out that if we attempt to live holy lives by keeping the law, we will find we can't be holy. Instead, we will be frustrated.

In Romans 7:7, we can see that Paul anticipated resistance to change, because he raised a question: "What shall we say, then? Is the law sin?"

Paul says, "Certainly not!" In fact, in verse 12, he points out that the law is holy, righteous, and good. Paul recognized that the minute he said, "Live by grace, not by law," a whole group of Christians would say, "Paul, are you suggesting the law is inferior? Are you suggesting that somehow it's inadequate, perhaps even sinful or evil?"

Paul says, "No, that's not what I'm suggesting." But he says, "What you do need to understand is why God gave the law. What was his intent?" So he says in the rest of verse 7, "Indeed I would not have known what sin was except through the law. For I would not have known what coveting really was if the law had not said, 'Do not covet.'"

Soon after babies are born, they begin to grow teeth. Once those teeth come, they begin to eat differently. However, there is often that youngster playing in the sandbox and right next to him is a nice, plump arm. And so the child reaches out and uses those new teeth. He eats just like he has eaten before. That's when the mother lays down a new law: "No—you can bite your food, but you can't bite Johnny. Didn't you notice how he cried when you bit him?"

Paul says that's what God did. God came to those who thought certain things they were doing were right or proper. But God's law didn't just deal with action.

It didn't just deal with things like lying or stealing or committing adultery. God's law also dealt with desires and feelings, those things that cause people to lie, to steal, to commit adultery. Through the law God says, "If you wonder what I'm like, if you want to know what pleases me, if you want to see a reflection of my character, don't covet, don't lie, don't steal. This is how you ought to live."

HOW DOES THE LAW CAUSE OUR DOWNFALL?

If the law reveals that God doesn't want people to lie, steal, and commit adultery, shouldn't that be enough? Shouldn't the law compel us to live holy lives?

Paul says there's another problem: the law runs into people who are controlled by sin. Romans 7:8-10 says, "But sin, seizing the opportunity afforded by the commandment, produced in me every kind of covetous desire. For apart from law, sin is dead. Once I was alive apart from law; but when the commandment came, sin sprang to life and I died. I found that the very commandment that was intended to bring life actually brought death."

I don't know about you, but when I read those verses, my question is, "Paul, what are you saying? You talk about sin being dead. You talk about sin springing to life. You talk about being dead to the law. You talk about coming to life. What are you talking about?"

Let me suggest this illustration. Have you ever noticed that when you go through orientation and training for a new job, they never tell you everything? There's always something they forget. As you're working, you're confronted with a situation that was not covered in orientation. You're tired of going back to your manager and asking questions. You don't want to look like a dummy. You want to show some initiative. So you attack that situation and you create a set of procedures that helps you quickly and efficiently finish the task. For the next two or three months, every time that situation arises, you do what you think is right.

Three months later, your manager comes by, observes what you're doing, and says, "That's the wrong procedure. You're going against company policy. What you're doing doesn't take into account what's happening in accounting or sales. You need to do it a different way. Here are the new procedures." You realize that in relationship to the company's policies, you've been sinning, not following the correct procedures.

But something else occurs the moment your manager tells you that. If you're like I am, something down here says, *Wait a minute! My manager doesn't understand my job. I figured it out. I've done it efficiently. If I follow my manager's procedures, it's going to be more paperwork, more bureaucracy.* And when the manager leaves, the temptation is to do it the way you've been doing it the last three months. Why? Because there's something deep inside of us that causes us to respond negatively to law.

God gave the law to man, saying: This is the way I want people to live. The apostle says that when people are controlled by sin and are confronted by the law, rather than changing and going back to God, we do just the opposite. We rebel. We won't live the way God wants. And we sin in greater and greater ways. God has all the evidence he needs, as if he needed more. When a sinner stands before him and the books are opened, God can say, "Here's my law; here's what you knew. Instead of coming to me, you went the other way." The evidence is marshaled, and we are condemned.

That's what Paul says in Romans 7:13: "Did that which is good, then, become death to me? By no means! But in order that sin might be recognized as sin, it produced death in me through what was good, so that through the commandment sin might become utterly sinful." That's why God gave the law to us: not to make us holy, not to make us righteous, but to show us that we are utterly sinful. And when an utterly sinful person sees his sin before the law, he moves the opposite way.

Some of you may be thinking, *Wait a minute. That may be the way the unbeliever responds to God's law, but why do we need to make a change? We've been born again. The control of sin in our life has been broken. God has given us the ability to live for him. Why does Paul say to us, "Make a change. Don't live by law; live by grace." Shouldn't we of all people be able to live holy lives by keeping the law?*

Paul shows us by way of personal illustration that that's impossible.

PAUL SAYS SOMETHING INSIDE OF HIM IS STILL A SLAVE TO SIN.

Romans 7:14 says, "We know that the law is spiritual; but I am unspiritual, sold as a slave to sin." In verses 15-18, he says, "I do not understand what I do. For what I want to do I do not do, but what I hate I do. And if I do what I do not want to do, I agree that the law is good. As it is, it is no longer I myself who do it, but it is sin living in me. I know that nothing good lives in me, that is, in my sinful nature. For I have the desire to do what is good, but I cannot carry it out." We need to realize that when God gave the law, the purpose was to show the utter sinfulness of sin. God never gave the law to make people holy. He gave the law so they would see they are sinners.

The minute we try to live holy lives by keeping the law, we go the opposite way. So the apostle says in verses 21-23: "I find this law at work: When I want to do good, evil is right there with me. For in my inner being I delight in God's law; but I see another law at work in the members of my body, waging war against the law of my mind and making me a prisoner of the law of sin at work within my members."

HOW DO WE BREAK FREE FROM THIS CYCLE?

Paul's dilemma—and mine—is that the law tells me what God wants, but every time I try to use the law to enable me to live a holy life, I do exactly the opposite. How frustrating! Paul describes himself as "a wretched man" (v. 24). What in the world can I do? The only answer Paul can come up with is to recognize I am a slave of Jesus Christ. And as a slave of Christ, "Don't live by the law.

When we live by the law, we will never be holy, only frustrated." The times in our lives when we have perhaps been most frustrated are when we have attempted to live for God by keeping the law.

My father was raised a Quaker. He learned from the time he could remember that our responsibility is to treat Sunday like Israel treated the Sabbath. That meant when you got up in the morning, you got dressed and went to meeting. When you came home, you stayed dressed and ate dinner. Then you had two options: either sit in the parlor and talk, or take a nap, two options that children love. You weren't allowed to play ball. You weren't allowed to go outside and get dirty. Why? Because this is the Sabbath and we must keep it this way.

The problem was that keeping that law doesn't produce holiness. All it produces is frustration.

There are parts of the Mosaic Law that you and I may latch on to because of our background, our heritage, because somehow we think that's what we're supposed to do. Whether it's what we eat, our tithe, or setting aside certain days, we're committed to it because we think that will produce holiness. And Paul says, "Every time I come back to the Law of Moses and try to live a holy life, it doesn't produce holiness, because I still have a sin nature. I saw the law telling me not to lie, and I lied. I saw the law telling me not to covet, but I coveted. I saw the law telling me not to be immoral, but I lusted."

The law can't produce holiness. That was never its purpose.

Some of you might say, "I don't live by the law of Moses." Let me suggest there are many of us who live under the "laws of application." One of the things we preachers do is take principles of Scripture and make them concrete and specific. We bring them by way of application into life, and after a while those things become laws.

I was raised in a church where it was communicated week after week that if you really wanted to be spiritual, you didn't show up just Sunday morning.

You went to Sunday school. You went to Sunday morning church. You went to Sunday evening church. And if you really wanted to be spiritual, you'd show up Wednesday night, because, as we were told, "The spiritual thermometer of the church is Wednesday night." You know what I learned? That's not true. You know how I learned it? Because I was there. And I didn't want to be there. I hated being there. And not just when my parents dragged me—I'm talking about when I became the pastor of a church, and people expected me to be there! I found it didn't produce spiritually. All it produced was frustration.

Some of you say, "I don't live under the laws of Moses, and I don't live under the laws of application." Then perhaps you've had to live under the "laws of the Pharisees," the kinds of things we do as Christians just like the Pharisees. If the cliff is here and the law says don't go over the cliff, we build the fence 50 feet back so that nobody gets near it. That's exactly what the Pharisees did.

The Bible says that lust is wrong. But if that is where the cliff is, we build the fence 50 feet back and say, "Don't you dare look at TV or go to movies. Only read *Forbes* and the *Wall Street Journal* so you can lust over money, but nothing else. We create these kinds of laws and somehow have the idea that if we can keep them, we will be holy, and God will be pleased with us.

It's always amazed me that those churches that have all of these rules and regulations have just as big a problem with immorality, with thievery, with gossip, with all of the sins of the Bible, as the churches that don't have those laws. Why? Because law was never intended to produce holiness. All that law was intended to do was to show man that he is a sinner.

Some of you might say, "Well, I don't struggle with the law of Moses. I don't even struggle with the law of application. I don't even know if I struggle with the law of the Pharisees. I'm from California; anything goes." I suggest that you probably have to struggle with what I call the "law of lifestyles."

God leads some Christians into a certain lifestyle, and it fits those Christians.

But then their desire is to make what they do a law for everyone else. And if we don't live and think exactly as they do, we're made to feel guilty.

Some Christians communicate to me that if I don't homeschool, I'm not walking with the Spirit; I really can't be pleasing God. Then other Christians say, "No, you've got to send your children to the Christian School, or you really don't know the mind of God." Then other Christians say we're to be salt and light, and if you don't have your child in a public school, then you don't know the mind of God. You really can't be pleasing God.

I hate to tell you this, but reading from Genesis to Revelation, I don't find a thing about "elementary" and "secondary" education in the Bible, including Deuteronomy 6. We need to realize that if something works for us, God says, "Fine, live that way. But if you want to make that a law for someone else, you're not going to make them holy. You're just going to make them frustrated."

There are a lot of books out on marriage and raising children, many of them good. But we need to realize they were written because they worked in one person's life, and it doesn't necessarily mean they're going to work in somebody else's. I remember a couple holding some marriage seminars and telling people you need to get up at six in the morning and read to your spouse. That will make yours a godly marriage. My spouse and I don't even want to talk to each other at six o'clock in the morning! We have a rule: No talking until after ten. And we'll call each other on the phone and make up for whatever we said before ten. That makes our marriage work.

God hasn't called us to set up laws for other people. The apostle said, "When God gave the law, 'Do not covet; do not steal; do not lie,' he gave this to show men they are sinners." And when sinful people see the law of God, they're not going to come to God. They are going to go the opposite direction. That's why Jesus Christ came and died, so that all they have to do is to believe.

As a parent, I have the right and the responsibility to discipline my children.

I have the right to establish laws and enforce them. But I recognize that as a parent, all I can guarantee is that my children will obey my laws as long as I'm in the room. But what I'm also concerned about is how my child will live and act when he is grown up, on his own. That's when I want my child to decide correctly for the right reason. I realize I can't produce that with law. Oh, I can produce obedience, up to a point, with law. But not when my child is an adult. That's why as a parent, I have had to learn that as the child grows, so grows his or her freedom to make decisions and live with the consequences. If I want to produce maturity in my children, I've got to give them freedom.

That's what our master, Jesus Christ, has done for us. He says, "I haven't called you to live by law. Instead I've called you to live by the principles of the New Testament. Some of you may do them this way; some of you may obey them a different way. But that's fine. Because in order to produce maturity, I want to give my slaves freedom."

But let me tell you, it's only in the setting of freedom that you see an adult come to worship service because he or she wants to be there, who is involved in a prayer meeting in the home because he wants to be there, who is willing week after week to walk into that jail and meet with that abused kid because she wants to be there. Then and only then can you say of that kind of person, "These people are truly slaves of Jesus Christ. They're living for the freedom he gives, but they are sold out to him."

That's what it means to live by grace. And Paul says we need to make a change. Not to live by law, but to live by grace.

Preaching the Prophets with Honor

In many churches, the least-preached part of the Bible is the prophetic literature. Few sermons draw from Zechariah, Nahum, or Amos.

by Elizabeth Achtemeier

The prophet loves God's people. The stereotype of prophetic preaching is making judgments and castigating people's sins. The image is too often of God and the preacher standing on one side against the sinful people in the pews on the other.

I used to teach seminary satellite courses. I remember one preacher who could not preach his way out of a paper bag. I worked with him and struggled to find out why he couldn't preach. It turned out that he hated his congregation. He said, "They're a bunch of egotistical jerks." His view was that he and God were on one side and the people were on the other.

But actually he was all alone. God was with the people!

The Lord loves his sinful folk, so the Lord's prophets love them too. Throughout the prophetic writings, Israel is, to be sure, always stubborn, stupid, blind, and whoring. "O worm Jacob," as Isaiah calls him (Isaiah 41:14). But Israel also is, in the prophetic writings, "precious and honored in my sight" (43:4) and God's chosen servant (see 41:9).

Because the prophets bear the word of God, they bear also God's love for his foolish children. To preach from the prophets rightly, we can never overlook the prophets' identification with their sinful people. The God of the prophets is not only a righteous judge; God is also redeemer and re-creator.

To be sure, the primary message of the pre-exilic prophets is one of radical wrath. In Jeremiah, the Lord details the people's wrongs, then he asks the prophet, "Should I not punish them for this? . . . Should I not avenge myself on such a nation as this?" (Jeremiah 5:9). God's dreadful answer is, "Yes, I shall. Israel has lifted up her voice against me. Therefore I hate her" (Jeremiah 12:8, paraphrase).

That verse always sends chills up my spine. What would it mean if God hated us? To turn Paul's statement in Romans 8 upside down, "If God be against us, who can be for us?"

Perhaps we have never made clear to our congregations that we also suffer daily under the wrath of a sovereign Lord. The breakdown of our communities, our pain and strife, our warfare, our hatreds, our destruction, and our death are not just the automatic effects of our blind wrongdoings. They are evidence of God subjecting us to the fire of his very real judgment.

But when we equate prophetic preaching only with judgmental preaching, we fail to recognize that the prophets all proclaim salvation as well.

When Israel's life hangs in the limbo of the exile and her future seems cut off, it is the prophets who proclaim that God is not through with his people. In Jeremiah 29:11, "'I know the plans I have for you,' declares the LORD, 'plans to prosper you and not to harm you, plans to give you hope and a future.'"

The prophet in ancient Israel was not primarily a teacher of ethics. The primary function of the prophet in Israel was to illumine where and when God was at work in his world.

In Isaiah 10, that prophet maintains God is at work in the ascendancy of the Assyrian Empire. In verses 5 and 6, God says, "Woe to the Assyrian, the rod of my anger, in whose hand is the club of my wrath! I send him against a godless nation, I dispatch him against a people who anger me." Isaiah is pointing out how God can be seen, even in the brutal judgment of Israel.

The worlds of national and international relations are seldom understood by our congregations as being influenced by the actions of God. Rather they see their fate and destiny resting in the hands of the politicians, the industrialists, the military. The populace holds its breath at the terror of that thought.

Imagine the story of Israel if the pharaoh of Egypt or Nebuchadnezzar of the Babylonian Empire had really been in charge—if God has nothing to do with influencing the destiny of nations.

We can't equate prophetic preaching only with judgmental preaching. The prophetic message can be preached in the world of small things as well as large. Maybe we need to start small as we try to illumine for our people just where and when God is at work.

It is prophetic preaching on a small scale and on the basis of the Word of God to remark on that dead bird lying outside in the church parking lot. "God knows it has died," you might begin, "because not a sparrow falls to the earth without your Father's will, Jesus says."

Such simple proclamations help a congregation regain awareness that earth, seas, and skies remain only by God's faithful sustenance. Prophetic preaching points every simple event to its deeper relation to the will of God.

THE PROPHET CANNOT BE CLAIMED BY ANY ONE GROUP

We must abandon our attempts to identify the prophets' proclamations with one of our social programs or sets of ethical principles. We must regain the freedom that the prophets knew in the Word of God.

According to Isaiah 6, Isaiah 40, and especially Jeremiah 23:18, the true prophet has stood in the heavenly council of the Lord to perceive and to hear his word, and is then sent forth to proclaim the word that God will act among his people.

I cannot help but wonder in our day if we leaders in the church have not lost that freedom. There is now a well-defined ideology of the left among the mainline clergy, as well as an ideology among the conservatives on the right. The reaction of church leaders to any public problem can be pretty well predicted by their ideology. Yet each camp claims that "our positions are both Christian and prophetic."

In other words, we have frozen the free word of the prophets into an ideology; the lively oracles of God that stood opposed to every human claim to absolute wisdom and power have themselves been made the servant of absolutist pretensions.

THE PROPHET CALLS FOR COMMUNION WITH GOD

The prophets continually insist that knowledge of the purpose and will of God is had only in intimate communion with him, a communion comparable to that of a loving wife with her husband or of an obedient son with his father. Proper interpretation of the prophets depends, as Jeremiah would put it, on circumcising the foreskins of our hearts. Or, according to Ezekiel, it depends on getting ourselves a new heart and a new spirit.

The call for a living relationship with God is the central demand of the prophetic literature, and it is, therefore, the key for all attempts to preach from the prophets' writings.

FIND SPIRITUAL FORMATION TOOLS
Christian at BibleStudies.com

BUILD AN EFFECTIVE MINISTRY with Small Groups.com

Inspiring
Life-Changing
Community

▶ Learn how to **start or re-start** both small groups and entire ministries

▶ Choose from thousands of **training tools, Bible studies, and free articles** from trusted leaders like Philip Yancey, Les and Leslie Parrott, and Larry Crabb

▶ Connect your group with a free and fun **social-networking tool**

▶ **Train yourself and your leaders** with invaluable assessments and orientation guides

▶ Downloadable resources are ready for **immediate use** and can be copied up to 1,000 times

▶ Join the **blog conversation** and share your small-group experiences

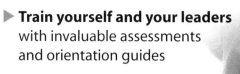

a service of

CHRISTIANITY TODAY
INTERNATIONAL

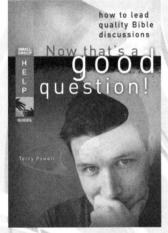

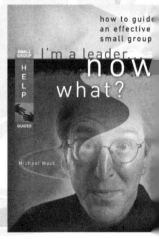